REVISE! "WUTHERING HEIGHTS" REVISION GUIDE

Anthony Markham

ANGRY SWAN PRESS
EDUCATIONAL BOOKS AND TEACHING AIDS

ANGRY SWAN PRESS

CONTENTS

Emily Brontë: A Biography

Emily Jane Brontë was born on July 30, 1818, in Thornton, near Bradford in West Yorkshire, England. She was the fifth of six children born to Patrick Brontë, an Irish Anglican clergyman, and Maria Branwell Brontë. Her siblings included Charlotte, Anne, Branwell, Elizabeth, and Maria. The Brontë family lived in Haworth, where Patrick served as the perpetual curate.

Emily's formal education began in 1824 when she and her three elder sisters were enrolled in the Clergy Daughters' School at Cowan Bridge in Lancashire. However, a tragic turn of events occurred when Maria and Elizabeth Brontë contracted tuberculosis at the school, leading to their deaths in 1825. Following this, Emily and her sisters were educated at home by their father.

Growing up in an environment of intellectual stimulation, Emily and her siblings developed a keen interest in literature. They created an imaginary world called Gondal, and Emily, along with Anne, wrote extensively about this fantasy realm. These early writings reflected the seeds of Emily's literary prowess.

In 1842, Emily attended the Pensionnat Héger, a boarding school in Brussels, with her sister Charlotte. Emily's experiences in Brussels influenced her writing, particularly her novel "Wuthering Heights."

Emily Brontë's literary legacy primarily rests on her only novel, "Wuthering Heights," published in 1847 under the pseudonym Ellis Bell. The novel, initially met with mixed reviews, is now considered a classic of English literature. Its dark and passionate exploration of love, revenge, and the supernatural set it apart from the literary norms of its time.

Emily's poetry also holds a significant place in her literary contributions. Although her poems were published posthumously, they showcase her distinct voice and emotional intensity.

Tragically, Emily Brontë's life was cut short by tuberculosis. She succumbed to the illness on December 19, 1848, at the age of 30. Her untimely death left a void in the literary world, and her reclusive nature contributed to the enigmatic aura surrounding her.

Despite her relatively brief literary career, Emily Brontë's impact on literature has been profound. "Wuthering Heights" is celebrated for its complex characters, innovative narrative structure, and the raw intensity of its themes. Her poetry, though fewer in quantity, is equally lauded for its lyrical beauty and emotional depth.

Emily Brontë's life may have been short, but her literary contributions have left an indelible mark on English literature. Her exploration of the human psyche and the complexities of passion in "Wuthering Heights" continues to captivate readers, making her a revered figure in the literary canon. Emily's legacy endures not only through her written works but also through the enduring fascination with the mysterious and talented Brontë siblings who left an indelible mark on the world of letters.

Exploring the Historical Context of "Wuthering Heights"

"Wuthering Heights," the classic novel penned by Emily Brontë and published in 1847, is a timeless tale of passion, revenge, and societal constraints. To fully appreciate the depth and complexity of this literary masterpiece, it's crucial to delve into the historical context that shaped both the narrative and its characters.

The Brontës and the Victorian Era:

The Brontë sisters, Emily, Charlotte, and Anne, were born in the early 19th century in Yorkshire, England. Raised in the isolated parsonage of Haworth, they were largely shielded from the outside world but were keen observers of the social and political transformations of the Victorian era. This period, characterised by Queen Victoria's reign from 1837 to 1901, witnessed significant changes in industry, class structures, and societal norms.

Wuthering Heights as a Reflection of Social Upheaval:

"Wuthering Heights" is set against the backdrop of the Yorkshire moors, portraying the harsh and unforgiving landscape that mirrors the tumultuous social climate of the time. The novel spans several decades, encapsulating the impact of the Industrial Revolution and the resultant shift from agrarian to industrial societies.

The characters in Wuthering Heights, particularly Heathcliff, reflect the consequences of social mobility and the rigid class distinctions prevalent in Victorian society. Heathcliff's status as an orphan and his ambiguous ethnicity underline the prejudice and discrimination faced by those outside the established social order. His journey from a destitute outsider to a wealthy landowner is emblematic of the changing power dynamics in a society grappling with economic and social transformation.

Love and Relationships in the Victorian Era:

The romantic relationships portrayed in "Wuthering Heights" are deeply influenced by the societal norms and expectations of the Victorian era. The restrictions imposed by class, gender roles, and societal expectations play a central role in shaping the characters' fates. The tumultuous love affair between Heathcliff and Catherine Earnshaw challenges conventional notions of romance, as their connection transcends societal boundaries but is ultimately marred by societal pressures.

Religion and Morality:

The Victorian era was marked by a strong influence of religion and morality on societal norms. The characters in "Wuthering Heights" grapple with questions of morality and the consequences of their actions. The novel's exploration of themes such as redemption, forgiveness, and the supernatural reflects the moral quandaries of a society deeply rooted in religious values.

"Wuthering Heights" remains a poignant and enduring work not only for its compelling characters and intricate plot but also for its profound exploration of the historical context of the Victorian era. Through Emily Brontë's lens, readers are transported to a time of social upheaval, class struggles, and shifting moral landscapes. By understanding the historical backdrop, one can truly appreciate the richness and complexity of this literary classic that continues to captivate readers across generations.

Unveiling the Enigma: In-Depth Exploration of the Key Characters in "Wuthering Heights"

"Wuthering Heights" by Emily Brontë remains a literary gem that captivates readers with its intricate characters, passionate emotions, and haunting landscapes. In this extensive article, we embark on a journey into the lives of the key characters that populate this timeless tale, exploring their complexities, motivations, and the roles they play in shaping the narrative.

Heathcliff - The Brooding Antihero:

Heathcliff, perhaps the most enigmatic and iconic character in "Wuthering Heights," is a brooding antihero whose presence casts a shadow over the entire novel. Adopted by the Earnshaw family, his origins remain mysterious, adding an air of ambiguity to his character. Heathcliff's tumultuous journey from an abused orphan to a wealthy landowner is marked by a burning desire for revenge against those who wronged him, particularly the Earnshaws and the Lintons. His passionate and obsessive love for Catherine Earnshaw is both the driving force behind his actions and the source of his profound suffering.

Catherine Earnshaw - The Complex Heroine:

Catherine Earnshaw, Heathcliff's beloved, is a complex and conflicted character. Her passionate nature and rebellious spirit make her a central figure in the novel. Catherine's internal struggle between her love for Heathcliff and the societal expectations that pull her towards Edgar Linton forms the emotional core of the story. Her untimely death leaves an indelible mark on the characters and the plot, setting the stage for the haunting events that follow.

Edgar Linton - The Civilized Gentleman:

Edgar Linton, a contrast to the rugged and unpredictable Heathcliff, represents the refined and civilized society of the Victorian era. A member of the Linton family, he falls in love with Catherine Earnshaw and becomes a pawn in the intricate web of relationships. Edgar's character highlights the class divisions and societal expectations that govern the lives of the novel's protagonists. His juxtaposition with Heathcliff adds depth to the exploration of societal norms and the consequences of crossing class boundaries.

Isabella Linton - The Tragic Victim:

Isabella Linton, Edgar's sister, becomes entangled in the web of passion and revenge when she marries Heathcliff. Her character serves as a tragic victim of Heathcliff's vengeful schemes, experiencing a loveless and abusive marriage. Isabella's story underscores the destructive power of unchecked passion and the consequences of defying societal norms.

Nelly Dean - The Narrator:

Nelly Dean, the housekeeper at Thrushcross Grange, serves as the primary narrator of "Wuthering Heights." Her intimate knowledge of the characters and events provides readers with an insider's perspective. Nelly's narrative adds a layer of subjectivity to the storytelling, offering insights into the complex motivations and emotions of the characters. However, her role as a storyteller also raises questions about the reliability of her account and the influence of her own biases.

The key characters in "Wuthering Heights" are a tapestry of passion, revenge, and societal constraints. Heathcliff, Catherine Earnshaw, Edgar Linton, Isabella Linton, and Nelly Dean each contribute to the rich and multifaceted narrative, making the novel a timeless exploration of human nature and societal complexities. As we delve into the lives of these characters, we uncover the layers of emotion, desire, and tragedy that make "Wuthering Heights" a literary masterpiece that continues to resonate with readers across generations.

WRITING TECHNIQUES

Emily Brontë, a Victorian-era author, is celebrated for her groundbreaking novel "Wuthering Heights," a timeless classic that continues to captivate readers with its dark passion and untamed landscapes. Brontë's unique style and innovative techniques have left an indelible mark on the literary world. In this article, we will delve into the distinctive techniques that define Emily Brontë as an author.

1. Atmospheric Descriptions:

One of Brontë's signature techniques is her masterful use of atmospheric descriptions. Through vivid and evocative language, she transports readers to the desolate moors of Yorkshire, where the turbulent love story of Heathcliff and Catherine unfolds. The setting becomes a character in itself, mirroring the tumultuous emotions of the protagonists. Brontë's ability to infuse the landscape with an almost supernatural aura contributes to the novel's eerie and gothic atmosphere.

1. Unreliable Narrators:

Brontë employs the device of unreliable narrators to add complexity to her narrative. Lockwood and Nelly Dean, the primary storytellers in "Wuthering Heights," present subjective perspectives colored by their own biases and limitations. This narrative choice forces readers to question the reliability of the information presented, creating an enigmatic and mysterious tone throughout the novel.

1. Multi-generational Narrative Structure:

Unlike many novels of her time, Brontë's narrative structure is not linear but multi-generational. The story unfolds over several decades, spanning the lives of the Earnshaw and Linton families. This intricate temporal structure allows Brontë to explore the lasting impact of love, revenge, and societal constraints over generations, providing a nuanced and comprehensive view of her characters and their relationships.

1. Exploration of Psychological Realism:

Brontë delves into the complexities of human psychology with a keen and unflinching eye. The characters in "Wuthering Heights" are not mere caricatures but intricate studies in the depths of human emotion. Heathcliff's brooding and vengeful nature, Catherine's conflicting desires, and the psychological torment of characters like Hindley and Isabella are meticulously examined. Brontë's exploration of the darker aspects of the human psyche adds depth and realism to her characters.

1. Themes of Social Class and Isolation:

Emily Brontë, living in a society heavily stratified by class, weaves social commentary into her narrative. The stark contrast between the Earnshaws and the Lintons serves as a commentary on the rigid class structure of 19th-century England. Furthermore, the theme of isolation permeates the novel, with characters often separated by physical, emotional, or societal barriers, underscoring the loneliness and alienation experienced by individuals trapped within their social roles.

Emily Brontë's techniques as an author in "Wuthering Heights" are nothing short of revolutionary. Her atmospheric descriptions, use of unreliable narrators, multi-generational narrative structure, exploration of psychological realism, and poignant themes of social class and isolation collectively contribute to the enduring power and fascination of her work. Brontë's literary prowess has left an indelible legacy, inspiring generations of readers and writers to appreciate the artistry of her storytelling.

Mastering the Art of Effective GCSE Essay Writing

Achieving success in the General Certificate of Secondary Education (GCSE) demands not only a solid grasp of subject matter but also a proficiency in essay writing. Whether tackling literature, history, science, or any other subject, the ability to convey ideas coherently and persuasively is paramount. This article aims to unravel the nuances of effective GCSE essay writing, offering valuable insights and practical tips to empower students on their academic journey.

Understanding the Essay Structure:

The foundation of effective essay writing lies in understanding and adhering to a well-structured format. Essays typically consist of an introduction, body paragraphs, and a conclusion.

- Begin with a compelling hook to grab the reader's attention.
- Clearly state your thesis or main argument.
- Provide an overview of the key points to be discussed.

2. Body Paragraphs:
- Each paragraph should focus on a single point or idea.
- Start with a topic sentence that introduces the main point.
- Support your argument with evidence, examples, or quotes.
- Ensure a logical flow between paragraphs.

3. Conclusion:
- Summarize the key points without introducing new information.
- Reinforce the thesis statement.
- End with a thought-provoking or conclusive statement.

Research and Planning:

1. Thorough Research:
- Familiarize yourself with the subject matter through research.
- Utilize reputable sources to gather information.
- Take organized notes to facilitate easy retrieval during writing.

2. Planning:
- Develop a clear outline before you begin writing.
- Allocate time for each section to manage your time effectively.
- Consider the word limit and ensure concise, relevant content.

Crafting a Strong Thesis Statement:

A robust thesis statement serves as the backbone of your essay. It should be concise, specific, and directly address the essay prompt. This statement provides a roadmap for both the writer and the reader, guiding the essay's focus and ensuring coherence throughout.

Effective Language and Style:

1. Clarity and Precision:
- Use clear and straightforward language to convey your ideas.
- Avoid unnecessary jargon or overly complex sentences.

2. Varied Sentence Structure:
- Incorporate a mix of sentence lengths and structures to enhance readability.

3. Vocabulary:
- Demonstrate a rich vocabulary but use it judiciously.
- Ensure that your choice of words aligns with the formality of the essay.

Revision and Proofreading:

1. Revise for Content:
- Review your essay for coherence and logical progression.
- Ensure each paragraph contributes to the overall argument.

2. Grammar and Punctuation:
- Check for grammatical errors, punctuation, and spelling mistakes.
- Verify that verb tenses are consistent throughout the essay.

3. Peer Review:
- Seek feedback from peers or teachers for constructive criticism.
- Consider their perspectives to refine your essay further.

Conclusion:

Mastering effective GCSE essay writing is a skill that transcends individual subjects. By understanding the fundamental structure, conducting thorough research, crafting strong thesis statements, employing effective language and style, and dedicating time to revision, students can enhance their essay-writing prowess. As they navigate the challenges of GCSE examinations, these foundational skills will not only bolster academic success but also contribute to their broader intellectual development.

Mastering the art of essay writing is not only essential for success in GCSEs but also lays the foundation for effective communication and critical thinking in various aspects of life. By following the comprehensive guide outlined above, students can develop the skills necessary to craft compelling and well-structured essays that stand out in their examinations. Happy writing!

KEY THEMES IN "WUTHERING HEIGHTS"

"Wuthering Heights," written by Emily Brontë and published in 1847, stands as a literary masterpiece that delves into the complexities of human relationships, love, revenge, and the eerie connection between the living and the dead. The novel, set against the desolate backdrop of the Yorkshire moors, weaves a narrative that explores profound and enduring themes. Here, we delve into the key themes that permeate the haunting landscape of "Wuthering Heights."

1. Love and Obsession:

At the heart of "Wuthering Heights" lies an exploration of love in its most intense and destructive forms. The passionate yet tumultuous relationship between Heathcliff and Catherine Earnshaw exemplifies this theme. Their connection goes beyond the conventional notions of romance, delving into the realms of obsession and possession. The novel prompts readers to question the thin line between love and destructive fixation, showcasing how love, when consumed by obsession, can lead to tragic consequences.

2. Nature vs. Civilization:

The novel is set in a stark contrast between the desolate, natural beauty of the Yorkshire moors and the rigid societal norms of the civilized world. Wuthering Heights, with its isolated location and turbulent atmosphere, serves as a symbol of the untamed and primal aspects of human nature. Thriving on the moors, characters like Heathcliff and Catherine defy societal conventions, highlighting the tension between the wildness of nature and the constraints of civilization.

3. Revenge and Retribution:

Revenge is a driving force that courses through the veins of "Wuthering Heights." Heathcliff's vengeful pursuit, fueled by the mistreatment he suffered as a child, becomes a central theme. The narrative unfolds as a tale of vendettas, where characters inflict pain on one another as a form of retribution. This theme echoes the cyclical nature of revenge, portraying how the sins of one generation haunt the next.

4. Death and the Supernatural:

The boundary between life and death is blurred in "Wuthering Heights," adding an eerie supernatural element to the narrative. Ghostly apparitions, particularly that of Catherine's ghost haunting Heathcliff, serve as a manifestation of unresolved passion and tragedy. The novel suggests that the impact of love and vengeance transcends mortal existence, lingering in the supernatural realm.

5. Social Class and Inequality:

Social class distinctions play a crucial role in shaping the characters' destinies. The divide between the affluent Lintons and the impoverished Earnshaws underscores the harsh realities of social inequality. Heathcliff's ascent from a persecuted orphan to a vengeful master challenges the rigid class structures of the time, sparking a critique of societal norms.

"Wuthering Heights" stands as a testament to Emily Brontë's exploration of the human psyche, societal constraints, and the enduring power of love and vengeance. The novel's themes resonate across time, inviting readers to confront the complexities of human relationships and the intricate interplay between the natural and civilized worlds. As readers traverse the desolate moors and navigate the tempestuous relationships within the pages of "Wuthering Heights," they are confronted with a narrative that transcends the boundaries of its era, leaving an indelible mark on the literary landscape.Title: Unraveling the Depths: Key Themes in Emily Brontë's Wuthering Heights

Unleashing the Power of GCSE Revision Aids: A Comprehensive Guide

The journey through GCSEs is a crucial phase in a student's academic life. As the exams approach, the quest for effective revision strategies becomes paramount. One powerful ally in this pursuit is the use of GCSE revision aids. These aids come in various forms, offering versatile support to students aiming for success. In this article, we will delve into the world of GCSE revision aids, exploring their types, benefits, and how to integrate them seamlessly into your study routine.

Understanding GCSE Revision Aids

1. Flashcards and Mnemonics:

- Flashcards: Condensed and portable, flashcards are an excellent tool for quick review sessions. Summarize key facts, formulas, or vocabulary on one side, with explanations on the other. Test yourself regularly to reinforce memory.
    - Mnemonics: Transforming complex information into memorable acronyms or phrases can aid recall. Create mnemonics for lists, sequences, or formulas to make them more accessible during exams.

2. Mind Maps and Concept Diagrams:

- Mind Maps: Visual representation of interconnected ideas, mind maps are great for subjects with a lot of relationships, such as history or science. Create a central theme and branch out with key concepts, connecting related information.
    - Concept Diagrams: Similar to mind maps, concept diagrams focus on illustrating relationships and hierarchies. These aids can enhance understanding and simplify complex topics.

3. Online Resources and Apps:

- Educational Platforms: Explore online platforms offering interactive lessons, quizzes, and revision materials. Platforms like Khan Academy, BBC Bitesize, and

Quizlet provide subject-specific resources.

 - Revision Apps: Utilize apps designed for GCSE revision, providing a gamified and engaging approach. Apps like Gojimo and Seneca offer interactive quizzes and study plans tailored to exam specifications.

4. Past Papers and Practice Questions:

 - Past Papers: An invaluable resource, past papers allow students to familiarize themselves with the exam format, question types, and time constraints. Use them as mock exams, analyzing mistakes and refining strategies.

 - Practice Questions: Supplement past papers with additional practice questions. This aids in reinforcing understanding, identifying weak areas, and honing problem-solving skills.

5. Audio and Video Resources:

 - Podcasts and Audiobooks: Turn your commute or downtime into productive study sessions with educational podcasts or audiobooks. Auditory learning can complement visual methods, reinforcing concepts through multiple senses.

 - Educational Videos: Platforms like YouTube host an array of educational channels covering various subjects. Visual explanations can enhance comprehension and make challenging topics more accessible.

Benefits of GCSE Revision Aids

1. Enhanced Retention:

 - Multisensory Learning: Revision aids engage different senses, reinforcing information through varied channels.

 - Active Learning: Flashcards, mind maps, and interactive apps encourage active participation, enhancing retention.

2. Efficient Time Management:

 - Targeted Revision: Revision aids help focus on specific topics or areas, preventing time wastage on already mastered content.

 - Quick Review: Flashcards and concise notes facilitate swift reviews, maximizing study efficiency.

3. Increased Motivation:

- Gamification: Many revision apps incorporate gamification elements, turning the learning process into a more enjoyable and motivating experience.
    - Progress Tracking: Monitoring progress with revision aids provides a sense of accomplishment, motivating continued effort.

4. Adaptability:

- Customization: Revision aids can be tailored to individual learning preferences and pacing.
    - Flexibility: Portable aids like flashcards allow for on-the-go revision, adapting to various study environments.

Integrating GCSE Revision Aids into Your Study Routine

1. Identify Your Learning Style:
    - Understand whether you are a visual, auditory, or kinesthetic learner.
    - Choose revision aids that align with your preferred learning style to enhance effectiveness.

2. Create a Diverse Toolkit:

- Combine different aids for a well-rounded approach. For instance, use flashcards for quick recall and mind maps for conceptual understanding.
    - Experiment with various tools to identify what works best for each subject.

3. Set Realistic Goals:

- Break down your revision goals into manageable tasks.
    - Align specific revision aids with each goal, ensuring a targeted and structured approach.

4. Consistent Use:

- Incorporate revision aids into your daily routine.
    - Regularly revisit flashcards, mind maps, or apps to reinforce learning and prevent

forgetting.

5. Collaborative Learning:

- Explore group revision sessions where different aids can be shared and discussed.
    - Collaborative learning can provide new perspectives and enhance the effectiveness of revision aids.

in the quest for GCSE success, revision aids stand as formidable allies, offering diverse approaches to learning and retention. By understanding the types of aids available and integrating them strategically into your study routine, you can unleash their full potential. Remember, the key lies not only in the tools themselves but in how you wield them on your academic journey.

EXAMINATION TEST QUESTIONS

Question 1

Consider the significance of entrapment in Wuthering Heights.

[40 marks]

Question 2

1 3 Answer part (a) and part (b)

Part (a)

What different feelings do you have about Heathcliff in different parts of the novel?
How do you think Heathcliff's behaviour is affected by the society in which he lives?

and then Part (b)

How does Brontë present Heathcliff to make you feel as you do?

Write about:

□ your response to Heathcliff at different times

□ how Brontë presents Heathcliff to make you feel as you do. (24 marks)

OR

Question 14

1 4 Answer part (a) and part (b)

Part (a)

Write about the ways Catherine Earnshaw changes as she grows from child to woman in
the novel.

You should write about:

□ the changes in Cathy's attitudes and behaviour

□ the ways that Brontë presents these changes.

and then Part (b)

How do you think the changes in Cathy may be influenced by the society in which she lives? (24 marks)

QUESTION 3

Answer one question from this section.

Remember to support your ideas with details from the writing.
Either 5 Read this extract, and then answer the question that follows it:
After behaving as badly as possible all day, she sometimes came fondling to
make it up at night.
'Nay, Cathy,' the old man would say, 'I cannot love thee; thou'rt worse than thy
brother. Go, say thy prayers, child, and ask God's pardon. I doubt thy mother and I
must rue that we ever reared thee!'
That made her cry, at first; and then, being repulsed continually hardened her,
and she laughed if I told her to say she was sorry for her faults, and beg to be
forgiven.But the hour came, at last, that ended Mr Earnshaw's troubles on earth. He
died quietly in his chair one October evening, seated by the fire-side.
A high wind blustered round the house, and roared in the chimney: it sounded
wild and stormy, yet it was not cold, and we were all together – I, a little removed
from the hearth, busy at my knitting, and Joseph reading his Bible near the table
(for the servants generally sat in the house then, after their work was done.) Miss
Cathy had been sick, and that made her still; she leant against her father's knee,
and Heathcliff was lying on the floor with his head in her lap.
I remember the master, before he fell into a doze, stroking her bonny hair – it
pleased him rarely to see her gentle – and saying –
'Why canst thou not always be a good lass, Cathy?'
And she turned her face up to his, and laughed, and answered,
'Why cannot you always be a good man, father?'
But as soon as she saw him vexed again, she kissed his hand, and said she
would sing him to sleep. She began singing very low, till his fingers dropped from
hers, and his head sank on his breast. Then I told her to hush, and not stir, for fear
she should wake him. We all kept as mute as mice a full half-hour, and should
have done longer, only Joseph, having finished his chapter, got up and said that
he must rouse the master for prayers and bed. He stepped forward, and called him
by name, and touched his shoulder, but he would not move – so he took the
candle and looked at him.
I thought there was something wrong as he set down the light; and seizing the
children each by an arm, whispered them to 'frame upstairs, and make little din –
they might pray alone that evening – he had summut to do.'
'I shall bid father good-night first,' said Catherine, putting her arms round his

19

neck, before we could hinder her.

The poor thing discovered her loss directly – she screamed out –

'Oh, he's dead, Heathcliff! he's dead!'

And they both set up a heart-breaking cry.

I joined my wail to theirs, loud and bitter; but Joseph asked what we could be thinking of to roar in that way over a saint in Heaven.

He told me to put on my cloak and run to Gimmerton for the doctor and the parson. I could not guess the use that either would be of, then. However, I went, through wind and rain, and brought one, the doctor, back with me; the other said he would come in the morning.

Leaving Joseph to explain matters, I ran to the children's room; their door was ajar, I saw they had never laid down, though it was past midnight; but they were

calmer, and did not need me to console them. The little souls were comforting each other with better thoughts than I could have hit on; no parson in the world ever pictured Heaven so beautifully as they did, in their innocent talk; and, while I sobbed, and listened, I could not help wishing we were all there safe together.

(from Chapter 5)

How does Brontë make this such a moving and significant moment in the novel? [25]

Or 6 : Victim or Monster – Which of these views do you think more accurately describes Brontë's portrayal of

Heathcliff? [25]

KEY QUOTATIONS FROM "WUTHERING HEIGHTS"

In GCSE English Literature, the ability to recall and use quotations effectively is crucial for success. Whether you're analysing a poem, novel, or play, integrating well-chosen quotes into your responses demonstrates a deep understanding of the text. Here's a guide to help you remember and use quotations effectively in your GCSE English Literature exams.

1. Start Early:

Begin by familiarising yourself with the key quotes as you read the text. Early exposure makes the process of memorisation more manageable. Take note of quotes that encapsulate important themes, character traits, or significant events.

2. Use Memory Aids:

Employ mnemonic devices or memory aids to associate quotes with specific characters, events, or themes. Create acronyms, rhymes, or visual associations that link the quote to its context. These memory aids can serve as mental triggers during exams.

3. Context Matters:

Understand the context of each quote. Knowing the circumstances in which a character speaks or an event occurs helps in recalling the quote accurately. Think about the emotions, conflicts, or revelations associated with the quote to reinforce your memory.

4. Organise Quotes by Themes:

Categorise quotes according to themes, characters, or literary devices. Creating a thematic framework helps you recall quotes relevant to specific essay questions. This organisational approach aids in retrieving quotes efficiently during exams.

5. Flashcards and Repetition:

Create flashcards with the quote on one side and the relevant context on the other. Review these flashcards regularly to reinforce your memory.

QUOTATION ONE

"He shall never know I love him: and that, not because he's handsome, but because he's more myself than I am. Whatever our souls are made out of, his and mine are the same."

Arguably the most renowned quote from Wuthering Heights, this excerpt from Chapter 9 captures Catherine expressing her profound emotions for Heathcliff to the housekeeper, Nelly Dean.

Despite her evident intense feelings for Heathcliff, Catherine explicitly states her decision to marry the more socially acceptable Edgar Linton.

This quote highlights Catherine's distinctive perspective on love. Instead of a simple declaration of love for Heathcliff, she expresses that Heathcliff is "more myself than I am." Catherine's conception of love blurs the boundaries between herself and Heathcliff, which may not be advantageous.

Considering the novel's subsequent events, this selfless passion might be a cautionary theme that Brontë intends to convey rather than endorse. Interpreted in this manner, Brontë's supposedly "romantic" novel serves a less romantic purpose, offering readers a warning rather than celebration.

QUOTATION TWO

"If all else perished, and he remained, I should still continue to be; and if all else remained, and he were annihilated, the universe would turn to a mighty stranger."

This passage is extracted from Chapter 9, where Catherine shares her feelings with Nelly regarding Heathcliff and Edgar. Catherine acknowledges that her fondness for Edgar might vary over time, but her love for Heathcliff is asserted to be enduring. Interestingly, Catherine admits that even if the entire universe were erased, as long as Heathcliff persisted, she would endure through him—taking the notion of a "soul mate" to an extraordinary level.

Some argue that Catherine's choice to marry Edgar may stem from an unconscious apprehension of what she believes Heathcliff symbolises within her own psyche. In confronting Heathcliff, Catherine is compelled to scrutinise the potentially destructive impulses of human desire.

QUOTATION THREE

"I wish I were a girl again, half-savage and hardy, and free."

It is apparent by now that Catherine grapples with internal conflicts. In this excerpt from Chapter 12 of Wuthering Heights, she nostalgically contemplates the time before encountering the Lintons and, by extension, the "civilised" world. Catherine seems to be reflecting on whether the civilising influence of Thrushcross Grange impeded her from living a more "authentic" life with Heathcliff.

A recurring question for first-time readers of Wuthering Heights is why Catherine would be preoccupied with societal expectations and relinquish a life with Heathcliff. After all, this novel is set in the most secluded regions of England, where societal norms have minimal impact.

Brontë presents intricate inquiries here about the enduring conflict between our yearning for the civilising influence of culture (embodied by the Lintons/Thrushcross Grange) and our uncontrollable, often self-destructive passions (represented by Heathcliff/the moors).

QUOTATION FOUR

"If he loved with all the powers of his puny being, he couldn't love as much in eighty years as I could in a day."

Heathcliff makes this comment in Chapter 14 to "prove" his love for Catherine is greater than Edgar Linton's could ever be. If Heathcliff loves Catherine as much as he does, however, wouldn't it be nobler to let her go? Indeed, after witnessing all the suffering this "love" causes Heathcliff and those around him, readers might reasonably consider love to be a negative force in Brontë's novel.

Instead of inspiring selflessness, love drives Heathcliff down a path of obsessive revenge.

QUOTATION FIVE

"Catherine Earnshaw, may you not rest as long as I am living. You said I killed you—haunt me then. The murdered do haunt their murderers. I believe—I know that ghosts have wandered the earth. Be with me always—take any form—drive me mad. Only do not leave me in this abyss, where I cannot find you! Oh, God! It is unutterable! I cannot live without my life! I cannot wi thout my soul!"

Heathcliff's intensity of emotion is so profound that certain readers find it challenging to perceive him as merely a human being. Instead, literary critics posit that Heathcliff embodies the formidable force of the untamed, natural world. Some go even further, suggesting that Heathcliff serves as a symbolic representation of Satan, embodying a disruptive and chaotic force justified by his own nature.

In this interpretation, Heathcliff transcends conventional human characteristics, becoming a symbol of the primal and unrestrained aspects of existence. This perspective invites a broader exploration of his character, associating him not only with the tumultuous forces of nature but also with archetypal representations of malevolence and disruption in the literary realm. Heathcliff, thus, takes on a multifaceted significance, embodying both the untamed aspects of the natural world and the symbolic embodiment of a disruptive, self-justified force akin to Satan.

QUOTATION SIX

"I have not broken your heart — you have broken it; and in breaking it, you have broken mine."

Author Virginia Woolf's analysis of Jane Eyre and Wuthering Heights may shed light on the recurring theme of a "fused identity" between Catherine and Heathcliff in the latter novel. In contrast to Jane Eyre, Woolf contends that Wuthering Heights lacks a distinct "I." According to her, Emily Brontë, rather than articulating personal aspirations, sought to convey a more "general conception" in her writing, distinct from her sister's approach. Instead of expressing simple sentiments like "I love" or "I hate," Woolf suggests that Brontë's main characters address their remarks to "the whole human race" or "the eternal powers."

This interpretation offers insight into the ambivalence experienced by both Catherine and readers towards Heathcliff. Despite the surface repulsion provoked by many of Heathcliff's actions, there is an acknowledgment that he embodies a primal truth universally experienced: frustrated desire. In this context, Heathcliff transcends the confines of his individual ego; he becomes a representative of a broader, universal truth within Brontë's cosmic drama.

By adopting Woolf's perspective, the conflicted emotions surrounding Heathcliff become more comprehensible. Readers may find themselves simultaneously repelled and drawn to Heathcliff, recognising in him a reflection of their own encounters with thwarted desires. This dual response reflects the tension between the individual and the universal, encapsulating the broader human experience of grappling with primal emotions. In essence, Woolf's insights illuminate a profound layer of Wuthering Heights, suggesting that Brontë's characters serve as conduits for expressing universal truths rather than mere individual experiences. This approach invites readers to delve into the cosmic dimensions of the narrative, where the characters transcend their personal narratives to embody broader, timeless realities within the human condition.

QUOTATION SEVEN

"I gave him my heart, and he took and pinched it to death; and flung it back to me. People feel with their hearts, Ellen, and since he has destroyed mine, I have not power to feel for him."

Encountering Wuthering Heights quotes such as this one from Catherine may prompt readers to speculate about the extent to which Emily Brontë drew inspiration from personal romances in her novel. Intriguingly, despite the novel's intense exploration of love and passion, Emily Brontë herself never married, leading a remarkably secluded existence amid the windswept Yorkshire moors. Consequently, the vibrant and memorable characters within Wuthering Heights appear to have sprung entirely from the fertile soil of Brontë's imaginative prowess.

Notably, there is a notable exception in the form of Catherine's brother, Hindley, who might have some roots in reality. Biographers posit that Brontë may have partially based Hindley on her own brother, Branwell. Parallels emerge as both characters face a descent into alcoholism. In the novel, Hindley turns to drink as a means of solace following the death of his wife, Frances, whereas Branwell's struggles with alcohol seem entwined with a passionate entanglement with a married woman.

This glimpse into the potential real-life inspiration behind Hindley adds a layer of complexity to Brontë's character creation. It underscores the nuanced interplay between the author's imaginative genius and her familial experiences, offering a bridge between the fictional realm and the author's personal reality. Despite this connection, the majority of Wuthering Heights' characters continue to emerge as products of Brontë's creative mind, contributing to the novel's enduring allure and enigmatic charm.

QUOTATION EIGHT

"I am now quite cured of seeking pleasure in society, be it country or town. A sensible man ought to find sufficient company in himself."

While discussions about Wuthering Heights often revolve around Heathcliff and Catherine, it is crucial to acknowledge Emily Brontë's primary narrator, Lockwood. The choice of Lockwood as the narrative voice might initially puzzle readers, but one theory suggests that Brontë strategically employs Lockwood as a foil to Heathcliff.

In the provided quote, Lockwood presents himself as a "sensible man" who relishes the solitude's splendors, yet his actions consistently betray an awkward desire for attention. Despite his professed enjoyment of solitude, Lockwood inadvertently carries the affectations of "society" with him into the untamed moors. This starkly contrasts with Heathcliff, who likely possesses a more profound understanding of genuine solitude than Lockwood has ever encountered.

Furthermore, Lockwood diverges significantly from Heathcliff in terms of emotional expression. While Heathcliff is known for his intense passions, Lockwood grapples with serious issues of emotional repression. Notably, Lockwood confesses to withdrawing "icily into [himself], like a snail" when faced with advances from a young woman in a seaside town. Thus, in contrast to Heathcliff's unrestrained expression of emotions, Lockwood's passions remain tightly locked within.

The juxtaposition between Lockwood and Heathcliff not only serves to highlight the complexities of the characters but also underscores the broader themes within the novel. Lockwood's presence introduces an element of societal norms and emotional repression into the wild moors, offering readers a contrasting perspective to Heathcliff's unrestrained passion and solitary existence. This narrative dynamic enriches the layers of Wuthering Heights, prompting readers to explore the interplay between societal conventions and the untamed forces that shape the characters and their relationships.

QUOTATION NINE

"I'm wearying to escape into that glorious world, and to be always there: not seeing it dimly through tears, and yearning for it through the walls of an aching heart: but really with it, and in it."

In the twilight of her existence, Catherine shares with Nelly her aspiration to transcend into a "glorious world," prompting an intriguing exploration into the nature of this envisioned realm. While it might be tempting to interpret this "glorious world" as a reference to heavenly salvation, the complexities of Wuthering Heights defy easy categorization within the confines of a Christian narrative. Instead, the novel encompasses spiritual and supernatural elements that elevate the story beyond conventional religious interpretations. Notably, Catherine's profound awareness of the pervasive force of nature, epitomized by Heathcliff and the expansive moors, adds a layer of mysticism to the narrative. Within the novel, there are glimpses of an enigmatic "power" or, perhaps, a perception of eternity that Catherine seems to apprehend. Although Emily Brontë doesn't explicitly articulate her metaphysical beliefs in Wuthering Heights, the enduring power of the novel appears to stem from its intricate exploration of the mysteries of nature and the profound essence of human existence.

Wuthering Heights stands apart as a work that delves into the nebulous intersection between the tangible and the supernatural. Rather than adhering to a rigid religious framework, the narrative embraces the ambiguous, inviting readers to ponder the profound forces at play in the characters' lives. This complexity contributes to the enduring appeal of the novel, as it challenges readers to grapple with the enigmatic aspects of nature and the potent influence of humanity's essence. In essence, Wuthering Heights' enduring allure is intricately tied to its nuanced reflections on the mysterious nature of the world and the profound power embedded in the human experience. Brontë's deliberate ambiguity allows readers to explore the novel's rich tapestry of ideas, leaving room for individual interpretation and contributing to its status as a timeless and captivating literary work.

QUOTATION TEN

"It was not the thorn bending to the honeysuckles, but the honeysuckles embracing the thorn."

Within the excerpt from Chapter 10, the term "thorn" symbolically represents Catherine, while the "honeysuckle" alludes to the civilizing impact of Thrushcross Grange. The Lintons, with their refined sensibilities, embark on the transformative journey of converting this wild "thorn" from the moors into a cultivated lady, introducing her gradually to the refined nuances of society. This metamorphosis is emblematic of the civilizing force that the Lintons bring into Catherine's untamed existence. Nevertheless, echoes of Catherine's reservations about the advantages of transitioning from the moors to the Lintons' societal realm resonate in previous quotes. The juxtaposition between the wild, unrestrained moors and the cultivated refinement of Thrushcross Grange encapsulates a tension within Catherine. While the Lintons aim to mold her into a proper lady, the moors represent an untamed authenticity that Catherine appears hesitant to relinquish.

This intricate interplay highlights the internal conflict faced by Catherine as she grapples with the dualities of her existence. The quote serves as a window into the complex dynamics of societal refinement and the inherent tension between embracing civilization and retaining the wild authenticity of one's origins. Catherine's reluctance suggests a profound connection to the moors, raising questions about the true benefits and costs of societal assimilation.

In essence, this passage contributes to the broader exploration of themes within Wuthering Heights, inviting readers to contemplate the impact of societal influences on individual identity. The symbolism of the "thorn" and "honeysuckle" underscores the tension between the wild and the refined, providing a lens through which the novel delves into the intricate complexities of societal transformation and personal authenticity.

QUOTATION ELEVEN

"I have dreamt in my life, dreams that have stayed with me ever after, and changed my ideas; they have gone through and through me, like wine through water, and altered the color of my mind. And this is one: I'm going to tell it — but take care not to smile at any part of it."

While Wuthering Heights is commonly perceived as a romance, it is essential to acknowledge the numerous Gothic elements skillfully incorporated by Emily Brontë. Among these elements, the extensive use of dreams stands out prominently.

In the provided excerpt from Wuthering Heights, Catherine articulates the profound impact that dreams have left on her psyche, stating that they have "altered the colour of [her] mind." Catherine appears particularly attuned to the enigmatic realm of the psyche. Regrettably, her heightened sensitivity to this aspect contributes to her untimely demise, succumbing to a "brain fever."

QUOTATION TWELVE

"Catherine Earnshaw, may you not rest as long as I am living. You said I killed you – haunt me then. The murdered do haunt their murderers. I believe – I know that ghosts have wandered the earth. Be with me always – take any form – drive me mad. Only do not leave me in this abyss, where I cannot find you! Oh, God! It is unutterable! I cannot live without my life! I cannot live without my soul!"

Should Heathcliff find himself unable to claim Catherine as his wife, he is prepared to embrace the morbid alternative of being her murderer, subjecting himself to eternal torment by the haunting specter of Catherine's ghost. This stark scenario vividly illustrates the twisted transformation of what is commonly perceived as "love" for another human being.

Following Catherine's demise, Heathcliff descends into an unsettling obsession with her lifeless form. He confides in Nelly, revealing that he senses Catherine's ghostly presence and derives a peculiar comfort from the sight of her deceased body. This disturbing fixation underscores the depth of Heathcliff's emotional turmoil and the distorted nature of his connection with Catherine.

The veracity of Catherine's ghost, however, remains a subjective matter for each reader of Wuthering Heights to ponder and decide. The novel leaves this haunting ambiguity, challenging readers to grapple with the supernatural elements interwoven with the complex and often disturbing relationships depicted in the narrative.

QUOTATION THIRTEEN

"A person who has not done one half his day's work by ten o'clock, runs a chance of leaving the other half undone."

In the concluding moments of Chapter 7, Nelly Dean reproaches Lockwood, discouraging further inquiries into Wuthering Heights' tumultuous history. While Lockwood expresses a desire to delve deeper into the past, Nelly, embodying her more conservative and God-fearing character, urges the new guest to prioritise a good night's rest, anticipating a full day of work ahead.

This incident serves as a poignant illustration of Nelly Dean's character and her adherence to conventional values. It is imperative for readers to recognise that the entire narrative of the Earnshaw-Linton saga is channelled through the lens of Nelly Dean's value system. This perspective prompts readers to scrutinise Nelly's responses, or lack thereof, to the violent incidents unfolding within the novel. Some critics go to the extent of labelling Nelly Dean as the "villain" of Wuthering Heights, highlighting the potential consequences of her conservative beliefs.

A pertinent question emerges: does Emily Brontë employ the characterisation of Nelly Dean to critique traditional piety? The narrative challenges readers to contemplate whether Nelly's staunch adherence to conventional values reflects a broader commentary on the limitations and shortcomings of traditional religious and moral frameworks. Brontë's exploration of Nelly Dean's character invites readers to ponder the complexities of morality, religious dogma, and the consequences of rigid adherence to societal norms.

QUOTATION FOURTEEN

"I have to remind myself to breathe – almost to remind my heart to beat!"

While Heathcliff professes a lack of fear towards death, he concedes to Nelly Dean that he finds himself unable to endure his present state. In a moment of vulnerability, Heathcliff discloses his innermost sentiments, expressing a desire for the culmination of the enduring struggle that has defined his life. He articulates to Nelly that he wishes the prolonged battle he has been engaged in could reach its conclusion.

This revelation provides a glimpse into the profound internal conflicts plaguing Heathcliff, showcasing a complex interplay between his apparent fearlessness towards death and the weariness that pervades his existence. The statement alludes to the intricate emotional landscape that Heathcliff navigates, hinting at a weariness that transcends the physical realm, delving into the realm of the existential and spiritual. Heathcliff's confession adds depth to his character, portraying him as a figure grappling with internal strife and longing for a resolution to the enduring turmoil that has shaped his life.

QUOTATION FIFTEEN

"A wild, wicked slip she was."

Let's be frank; the Wuthering Heights quote from Chapter 5 depicting Catherine as a young girl doesn't particularly stand out. It essentially provides a straightforward portrayal of Catherine in her youth. However, its significance lies in being one of the most frequently misattributed quotes within Wuthering Heights.

For those who have perused popular websites in search of Wuthering Heights quotes, the phrase "She burned too bright for this world" may sound familiar. Curiously, many attribute this quote to Emily Brontë's masterpiece, but scholars have scoured the text without success in finding such a sentence. The nearest approximation to this description of Catherine can be traced back to the quote from Chapter 5 mentioned above.

QUOTATION SIXTEEN

"Time brought resignation, and a melancholy sweeter than common joy."

Discovered within Chapter 17, this particular quote delineates the emotional state of Edgar Linton in the aftermath of Catherine's demise. At a cursory glance, the statement may appear paradoxical – after all, melancholy and joy are commonly perceived as diametrically opposed emotions. However, contemporary scientific research suggests an intriguing perspective: a balanced infusion of pessimism may, in fact, serve as a protective measure against the onset of depression.

In essence, the seemingly contradictory amalgamation of melancholy and joy in Edgar Linton's emotional experience after Catherine's death might be viewed through a lens that acknowledges the complexity of human emotions. This interpretation aligns with emerging scientific insights that propose a nuanced understanding of mental well-being, highlighting the potential benefits of a tempered pessimistic outlook in maintaining emotional resilience. Thus, the apparent paradox in Edgar's emotional state invites contemplation on the intricate interplay of emotions and the evolving understanding of mental health.

QUOTATION SEVENTEEN

"Treachery and violence are spears pointed at both ends; they wound those who resort to them worse than their enemies."

In Chapter 17 of Wuthering Heights, Isabella Linton articulates a moral decree during a heated exchange with Hindley. Regrettably, a pervasive trend is observed not only among various characters in the novel but also in the real world – the failure to adhere to such wisdom results in profound suffering for both the individuals themselves and those within their sphere of affection.

Isabella's moral pronouncement serves as a poignant reminder of the potential consequences of disregarding ethical considerations in interpersonal relationships. The resonance of her words extends beyond the confines of the novel, echoing the widespread tendency of individuals, both in literary narratives and reality, to neglect these guiding principles. The ensuing repercussions often manifest as significant anguish for not only the transgressors but also those entangled in the intricate web of their relationships.

This recurring theme prompts reflection on the enduring relevance of moral insights and their applicability in navigating the complexities of human connections. Isabella's declaration becomes a narrative touchstone, inviting readers to contemplate the far-reaching implications of actions driven by disregard for moral values, a contemplation that reverberates through both fictional worlds and the intricate tapestry of real-life relationships.

QUOTATION EIGHTEEN

"Honest people don't hide their deeds."

Several of Nelly's assertions in Wuthering Heights are characterized by an oversimplified outlook, offering a surface-level truth while neglecting the nuanced complexities beneath. Such statements often fail to account for the intricacies inherent in human behavior.

Consider, for instance, the common occurrence of individuals with commendable intentions who choose to conceal their benevolent actions. An apt illustration of this lies in those who anonymously contribute to charitable causes. While it is logical to presume that individuals with nefarious motives might seek to conceal their deeds, it is equally valid to acknowledge that individuals of integrity may also opt for discretion in certain instances, concealing their virtuous actions from the public eye.

This notion of "hiding one's deeds" extends beyond the pages of the novel, as evidenced by Emily Brontë's decision to publish Wuthering Heights under the pseudonym Ellis Bell. Here, the acclaimed author herself chose to obscure her identity, underscoring the idea that individuals, whether within the realm of fiction or reality, may sometimes opt for anonymity or secrecy for reasons that extend beyond malintent. These layers of complexity challenge simplistic perspectives, urging readers to explore the multifaceted nature of human actions and motivations.

QUOTATION NINETEEN

"I lingered round them, under that benign sky: watched the moths fluttering among the heath and harebells, listened to the soft wind breathing through the grass, and wondered how any one could ever imagine unquiet slumbers for the sleepers in that quiet earth."

Lockwood's concluding reflections transpire as he traverses the graves of Catherine, Heathcliff, and Edgar, evoking an eerie resonance reminiscent of the novel's inception. These closing sentiments, steeped in an almost nightmarish ambiance, prompt an existential inquiry: to what extent can we delineate the boundaries between reality and fantasy within the intricate tapestry of Wuthering Heights?

Much like the enigmatic opening of the narrative, Lockwood's parting words cast a shadow of uncertainty over the veracity of the events recounted. The reader is left grappling with the haunting possibility that the delineation between reality and fantasy within the narrative is nebulous, a fluid continuum rather than a distinct demarcation. The haunting quality of these final observations invites contemplation on the illusory nature of truth in a tale saturated with passion, revenge, and spectral echoes.

The narrative's journey, from its commencement to Lockwood's concluding musings, becomes a labyrinthine exploration of the human psyche and the malleability of perception. The reader is compelled to question the authenticity of the characters' experiences and ponder the extent to which their actions are grounded in tangible reality or shrouded in the phantasmagoria of their own creation. In essence, the novel's denouement leaves us suspended in a realm where the boundary between reality and fantasy dissolves, inviting us to navigate the murky waters of subjective interpretation.

QUOTATION TWENTY

"I was frightened, and Mrs. Earnshaw was ready to fling it out of doors: she did fly up, asking how he could fashion to bring that gipsy brat into the house, when they had their own bairns to feed and fend for?"

A persistent question that captivates readers delving into the intricate narrative of Wuthering Heights revolves around the motivation behind Mr. Earnshaw's decision to bring Heathcliff from Liverpool to the desolate moors. Was this act merely an expression of Christian charity, or does it conceal a more ominous undertone?

Certain critics propose a provocative theory that posits Heathcliff as the potential offspring of an extramarital affair involving Mr. Earnshaw, providing a plausible explanation for Mrs. Earnshaw's vehement aversion to the newcomer. The insinuation of Heathcliff's possible familial ties adds a layer of intrigue, unveiling a potential hidden dimension to the enigmatic dynamics within Wuthering Heights.

Yet, as the narrative weaves its complex tapestry, it introduces a discomforting facet that some readers may prefer to sidestep—the specter of incestuous undertones between Catherine and Heathcliff. The unsettling notion that these characters, initially raised as quasi-siblings, later aspire to a romantic connection challenges conventional sensibilities. Some critics extend this disquiet to propose the intriguing idea that Emily Brontë may have channelled suppressed and taboo sexual feelings for her brother Branwell into the narrative, particularly in the 20th century with the rise of Freudian psychoanalysis.

However, it remains imperative to acknowledge that, despite the exploration of these contentious themes, the text steadfastly withholds definitive answers. Wuthering Heights, with its narrative subtleties and ambiguous intricacies, leaves these questions hanging in the literary ether, inviting readers to grapple with the uncertainties surrounding the characters' origins and the unsettling intimations woven into the fabric of their relationships.

QUOTATION TWENTY-ONE

**"It is hard to forgive, and to look at those eyes, and feel those wasted hands,'
he answered. 'Kiss me again; and don't let me see your eyes! I forgive what you
have done to me. I love my murderer—but yours! How can I?"**

Discovering forgiveness within the dark tapestry of Wuthering Heights proves to be a formidable challenge. While Heathcliff ostensibly professes forgiveness towards Catherine in a particular quote, the narrative unfolds a starkly contrasting tale through his actions. It becomes apparent that Heathcliff, much like several other characters, is propelled more by a thirst for vengeance than a selfless devotion born of love.

However, amidst the prevailing gloom, a glimmer of genuine hope emanates from the relationship between the young Cathy and Hareton Earnshaw. These two offspring, bearing both physical and psychological echoes of their progenitors, manage to transcend the shadows of their lineage. In contrast to the prevalent theme of vengeance, Cathy and Hareton exemplify the potential for forging connections founded on mutual respect and compassionate understanding.

This redemptive arc in the narrative serves as one of the few beacons of optimism in Wuthering Heights. By depicting Cathy and Hareton's ability to rise above the legacy of their forebears, Emily Brontë propounds a powerful theme – that our actions, rather than the decisions of our ancestors, wield the defining influence on our destinies. In this portrayal, Brontë suggests that the potential for redemption lies within the choices we make, providing a counterpoint to the pervasive cycle of vengeance that permeates much of the novel.

QUOTATION TWENTY-TWO

"...for what is not connected with her to me? and what does not recall her? I cannot look down to this floor, but her features are shaped in the flags! In every cloud, in every tree—filling the air at night, and caught by glimpses in every object by day—I am surrounded with her image! The most ordinary faces of men and women—my own features—mock me with a resemblance. The entire world is a dreadful collection of memoranda that she did exist, and that I have lost her!"

In this poignant soliloquy, Heathcliff lays bare the profound and all-encompassing impact that Catherine Earnshaw has etched upon every facet of his existence. His words unveil an overwhelming connection, an inextricable link between his very being and the essence of Catherine. To Heathcliff, every element of his surroundings, from the very floor beneath his feet to the celestial formations above, bears the indelible imprint of Catherine's presence.

The physical world transforms into a poignant tapestry, each thread woven with memories of Catherine. The floor, seemingly mundane, becomes a canvas where her features are intricately etched, an inescapable reminder of her existence. Every cloud that graces the sky and every tree that adorns the landscape becomes a vessel for her memory, filling the air with an ethereal resonance that envelops Heathcliff day and night.

The haunting beauty of Catherine's image lingers in the ordinary faces of men and women, even in Heathcliff's reflection. The very mirror of his own features becomes a source of torment as it reflects a resemblance that serves as both a solace and a reminder of the irrevocable loss. The entire world, as Heathcliff perceives it, transforms into a repository of memories, a vast collection of memoranda attesting to the existence of Catherine and the unbearable void left in her absence.

Heathcliff's words encapsulate the profound grief and obsessive longing that define his existence. The world becomes a reflection of his internal landscape, saturated with the melancholic echoes of a love that transcends the boundaries of time and space. In this poignant confession, Emily Brontë captures the essence of Heathcliff's despair and the enduring power of a love that refuses to be extinguished even in the face of death.

QUOTATION TWENTY-THREE

"He's more myself than I am. Whatever our souls are made of, his and mine are the same; and Linton's is as different as a moonbeam from lightning, or frost from fire."

In this evocative declaration, Catherine Earnshaw encapsulates the profound and transcendent nature of her connection with Heathcliff. Her words resonate with an intimate understanding that goes beyond the physical and extends into the very fabric of their souls. The comparison she draws between Heathcliff and herself surpasses conventional notions of shared experiences or common interests; it delves into the metaphysical essence of their beings.

Catherine's assertion that Heathcliff is "more myself than I am" suggests a merging of identities, a unity that transcends individual boundaries. The enigmatic and indefinable quality of the soul becomes the focal point of their connection. Catherine poetically expresses that whatever constitutes the essence of their souls is not merely similar but identical. The bond between them is not contingent on external circumstances or fleeting emotions; it is rooted in a shared essence that defies rational explanation.

The juxtaposition of their connection with that of Linton serves to accentuate the depth of Catherine's sentiments. She employs vivid metaphors, comparing the dissimilarity between Heathcliff and Linton to the stark contrast between a moonbeam and lightning, or frost and fire. These images vividly convey the vast chasm that separates the profound connection with Heathcliff from the superficial and ephemeral nature of her association with Linton.

Through Catherine's eloquent words, Emily Brontë explores themes of soulmate connection, destiny, and the irresistible pull of kindred spirits. The imagery evoked by the moonbeam, lightning, frost, and fire serves to paint a rich and nuanced picture of the stark disparities in the relationships Catherine experiences. Ultimately, this poignant expression encapsulates the depth of love and connection that transcends the physical realm, leaving an indelible mark on the hearts and souls of both characters in Wuthering Heights.

QUOTATION TWENTY-FOUR

"My love for Linton is like the foliage in the woods: time will change it, I'm well aware, as winter changes the trees. My love for Heathcliff resembles the eternal rocks beneath: a source of little visible delight, but necessary."

In this poetic comparison, Catherine Earnshaw eloquently delineates the contrasting nature of her love for two pivotal figures in her life, Linton and Heathcliff. The metaphors she employs vividly illustrate the ephemeral and transient quality of her affection for Linton, juxtaposed against the enduring and indispensable nature of her love for Heathcliff.

Catherine's likening of her love for Linton to the foliage in the woods carries an inherent acknowledgment of the changing seasons. The foliage, vibrant and lush in the woods, undergoes transformations with time, much like her love for Linton is expected to evolve. The analogy of winter changing the trees suggests an inherent transience, a recognition that the initial fervor and vibrancy of her affection may wane over time.

In stark contrast, her love for Heathcliff is metaphorically compared to the eternal rocks beneath. The rocks, unyielding and steadfast, stand as a timeless foundation, providing constancy amid the changing seasons. This comparison reflects the enduring and unchanging nature of her connection with Heathcliff, portraying it as a source of stability and necessity.

The choice of the word "necessary" to describe her love for Heathcliff adds a layer of complexity to the sentiment. It suggests that her love for Heathcliff goes beyond mere emotional attachment; it is an intrinsic and fundamental aspect of her being. The rocks, though not immediately associated with visible delight, symbolize a profound and indispensable force in her life.

Catherine's eloquent dichotomy between the evolving foliage and the eternal rocks captures the essence of her relationships with Linton and Heathcliff. It delves into the intricate dynamics of love, acknowledging its mutability while highlighting the enduring and essential aspects that define true, lasting connections. This passage, rich in metaphorical depth, contributes to the nuanced exploration of love and relationships in the intricate tapestry of Wuthering Heights.

QUOTATION TWENTY-FIVE

"My love for Linton is like the foliage in the woods: time will change it, I'm well aware, as winter changes the trees. My love for Heathcliff resembles the eternal rocks beneath: a source of little visible delight, but necessary."

In this profound analogy, Catherine Earnshaw draws an intricate comparison between her love for two significant figures in her life, Linton and Heathcliff. The use of nature-inspired metaphors not only adds richness to her expression but also unveils the complex nuances of her emotions.

Catherine's depiction of her love for Linton as resembling the foliage in the woods evokes a vivid image of transient beauty and cyclical change. The foliage, lush and vibrant during certain seasons, undergoes inevitable transformations with time, akin to the way her affection for Linton is subject to the ebb and flow of temporal shifts. The reference to winter changing the trees hints at the inherent temporality of her feelings for Linton, suggesting that as time progresses, the initial fervor may undergo alterations.

Contrastingly, her love for Heathcliff is likened to the eternal rocks beneath, invoking an image of unwavering strength and enduring stability. The rocks, though devoid of immediate visible delight, serve as a metaphor for a constant and foundational presence in her life. This portrayal of Heathcliff as the "eternal rocks" suggests a love that transcends the fleeting pleasures associated with the changing seasons. Instead, it becomes a bedrock, a source of unwavering support and necessity.

The choice of the word "necessary" to describe her love for Heathcliff adds a layer of depth to the sentiment. It implies that her connection with Heathcliff goes beyond transient emotions and superficial delights. Rather, it is an essential and fundamental component of her existence, contributing to the very core of her being.

This poignant analogy encapsulates the intricate nature of love and relationships, navigating the complexities of temporal changes and enduring foundations. Catherine's words serve as a lens through which readers can explore the temporal nature of emotions and the steadfastness of connections that withstand the test of time in the haunting landscape of Wuthering Heights.

Printed in Great Britain
by Amazon

39714661R00030